How do Baby Animals Learn?

Bobbie Kalman

Crabtree Publishing Company

www.crabtreebooks.com

Created by Bobbie Kalman

For Olivia Tomaso, who loves books,
especially ones about baby bears and other baby animals

**Author and
Editor-in-Chief**
Bobbie Kalman

Editor
Kathy Middleton
Crystal Sikkens

Photo research
Bobbie Kalman

Design
Bobbie Kalman
Katherine Berti
Samantha Crabtree
    (logo and front cover)

Print and production coordinator
Katherine Berti

Prepress technician
Katherine Berti

Illustrations
Bonna Rouse: page 8

Photographs
Creatas: page 18 (top)
Digital Vision: page 9 (bottom left)
Dreamstime: pages 8, 24 (nursing)
iStockphoto: page 5 (top right)
Other images by Shutterstock

Library and Archives Canada Cataloguing in Publication

Kalman, Bobbie
    How do baby animals learn? / Bobbie Kalman.

(It's fun to learn about baby animals)
Includes index.
Issued also in electronic formats.
ISBN 978-0-7787-4077-3 (bound).--ISBN 978-0-7787-4082-7 (pbk.)

    1. Learning in animals--Juvenile literature.
2. Animals--Infancy--Juvenile literature.
I. Title. II. Series: It's fun to learn about baby animals

QL785.K35 2012   j591.5'14   C2011-907671-3

Library of Congress Cataloging-in-Publication Data

Kalman, Bobbie.
    How do baby animals learn? / Bobbie Kalman.
        p. cm. -- (It's fun to learn about baby animals)
    Includes index.
    ISBN 978-0-7787-4077-3 (reinforced library binding : alk. paper) --
ISBN 978-0-7787-4082-7 (pbk. : alk. paper) -- ISBN 978-1-4271-7889-3
(electronic pdf) -- ISBN 978-1-4271-8004-9 (electronic html)
    1. Competition (Biology)--Juvenile literature. 2. Animals--Infancy--Juvenile
literature. I. Title.

QH546.3.K35 2012
577.8'3--dc23
                                                2011046090

Crabtree Publishing Company

Printed in Canada/012012/MA20111130

www.crabtreebooks.com   1-800-387-7650

Published in Canada
Crabtree Publishing
616 Welland Ave.
St. Catharines, Ontario
L2M 5V6

Published in the United States
Crabtree Publishing
PMB 59051
350 Fifth Avenue, 59th Floor
New York, New York 10118

Published in the United Kingdom
Crabtree Publishing
Maritime House
Basin Road North, Hove
BN41 1WR

Published in Australia
Crabtree Publishing
3 Charles Street
Coburg North
VIC 3058

What is in this book?

How do you learn?

There are many things that you have learned since you were born. You learned to crawl, walk, talk, and ride a tricycle and bicycle. You learned some of these things on your own, and your parents taught you other things. Now you are also learning many things at school. You have learned how to read and write, and you are learning about the world.
What other things are you learning?

How did you learn to crawl and walk? Did you learn on your own, or did someone teach you?

Could the baby on the left ride a tricycle? Why or why not? When did you learn how to ride one?

Did you
learn to use
a laptop at
school or
at home?

When did you
learn to read?
Who taught you?

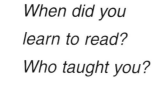

Why do you use
a **microscope**?
What do you see?

Can you play the
guitar? If you can,
how do you use your
hands to play it?

Can you ride
a skateboard?
If you can, how
did you learn?

How do you
learn about
the world
around you?

5

How do animals learn?

Animals cannot learn all the things that you can, but they do need to learn important things to keep themselves alive. How do they find food? How do they move and find their way? How do they stay safe? How do they "talk" to one another? How do baby animals learn to do all these things?

*A group of dolphins is called a **pod** or a **school**. What might baby dolphins learn from their school?*

How do baby animals move? Which body parts is this sloth using to climb trees and hang upside down? (See page 11.)

Where is this baby sea turtle crawling? Does its mother show it where to go? (See page 9.)

How do these baby meerkats keep safe from animals that hunt them? (See page 18.)

What are these young elephants doing? Are they dancing? (See page 21.)

How do baby animals know which foods to eat and where to find food? How does this baby fox learn to hunt? (See page 14.)

Animal mothers

Some baby animals are helpless when they are born or **hatch** from eggs. They need their mothers to feed them and keep them safe. Other babies are able to take care of themselves. They know what to do without being taught. Sea turtle babies, for example, know that they have to crawl to the ocean after they hatch.

sea turtle hatching

Mammals are animals with hair or fur, like these wolves. Mammal babies nurse, or drink milk made in the bodies of their mothers. Most mammal mothers care for their babies and teach them how to stay alive.

Mother sea turtles lay eggs in the sand on the same beach where they hatched. They then leave the eggs to hatch on their own.

When the babies hatch, they know they have to crawl across the beach to the ocean and swim away.

Many bird mothers, and some fathers, feed their baby birds and keep them warm and safe (see page 19).

After baby chipmunks stop nursing, they start living on their own. This baby is still with its mother, but it will soon leave her.

Learning to move

big feet

Most animals need to move to find food and keep safe. Special body parts allow them to move in different ways. Some walk or run, some hop or leap, some swim, and some fly. There are even animals that climb and hang upside down.

dolphin leaping

Bunny rabbits have strong back legs with big feet for hopping. Hopping allows them to move quickly.

__Foals__, or baby horses, can walk shortly after they are born.

hooves

Horses have __hooves__. Hooves help this mother and foal __gallop__, or run very fast.

Swans have webbed feet for swimming and wings for flying.

wings

webbed feet

These **cygnets**, or baby swans, are learning how to swim. Some of them are riding on their mother's back because they are tired, cold, or scared. Cygnets stay close to their parents for a year or two to learn skills like swimming and flying to faraway places.

claw

Sloths spend most of their time hanging upside down. They have **claws** with sharp toes for climbing and hanging. After they are born, they cling to the bodies of their mothers for a few months. This four-month-old sloth can climb and hang on its own.

What do they eat?

Animals need food and water to stay alive. They eat different kinds of food. **Herbivores** are animals that eat mainly plants. Herbivore mothers teach their babies how to find the right plants to eat. **Carnivores** are animals that eat other animals. **Predators** are carnivores that hunt the animals they eat. **Omnivores** eat both plants and other animals.

Animals need food and water.

Moose are herbivores. This mother moose is showing her calves which plants to eat. The calves stopped nursing at two months of age. They now eat many kinds of fruits, flowering plants, weeds, and the fresh, new leaves of trees.

This bobcat kitten is a predator. It has caught a chipmunk to eat. Turn the page to find out how predators learn to hunt.

Chimpanzees, or chimps, are omnivores. They eat fruit, leaves, seeds, flowers, honey, insects, and birds and their eggs. Chimpanzees will even hunt and eat small mammals, including monkeys and squirrels. Chimps are very smart mammals. They know how to use tools such as sticks and rocks. Chimpanzee mothers teach their babies how to use their fingers and thumbs to hold objects. This mother is teaching her baby how to grip with its thumb and fingers.

Learning to hunt

Predators hunt **prey**. Prey are the animals they eat. Baby predators need to learn how to hunt so they can stay alive. Some, like the baby eels on the next page, know how to hunt on their own. Others hunt with their mothers, who teach them to catch their prey in different ways.

fox pouncing

*These fox kits are hunting with their mother. They watch for prey and sniff the ground. When they find a mouse or rabbit, they **pounce**, or jump quickly on top of it. The kit on the left has caught a mouse to eat.*

This brown bear cub is learning how to catch fish. Its mother is nearby. Brown bears are omnivores that love fish!

Lion cubs practice their hunting skills by wrestling with each other. The top cub is growling to seem more scary!

These twin baby eels are fish that hunt other fish. They wait for fish to swim close to their underwater hole.

Why do they travel?

Many animals **migrate**. To migrate is to move from one area to another and then back again. Some animals migrate to warm places to get away from cold winters. Other animals migrate to lay eggs or have babies in other parts of the world. Migrating animals do not take ships or planes. They use their own **energy**, or strength, to travel. They find their way without maps. Sea turtles, some whales, and many kinds of birds migrate.

Humpback whales migrate from cold oceans to warm oceans, where their calves are born. The babies nurse from their mothers and then swim back with them to the cold oceans where whales can find food. The mothers teach their calves the way home.

tern chicks

The Arctic tern migrates farther than any other animal. Each year, terns make two long journeys. They fly from the North Pole to the South Pole and back again! Tern mothers lay eggs in the Arctic, near the North Pole. After the chicks hatch, they migrate with their parents as soon as they have learned how to feed themselves. The parents teach them where to fly and how to catch fish along the way.

Elephants eat huge amounts of grasses, bushes, and other plants to give their big bodies energy. They need to migrate to find enough food and water. An elephant family is led by its oldest and largest mother. She knows where to find food and water and leads the others there. Elephant calves need their mothers, as well as the other elephant mothers in the herd, to care for them and teach them how to find food and water.

How do they survive?

Baby animals need to know how to survive so that predators will not eat them. Some animals keep their babies safe in pouches on their bodies. Some hide their babies in **dens**, or homes. Other parents teach their babies to be on guard for predators. Baby animals must learn how to protect themselves from danger.

This cougar mother is taking her cub to a new den to protect it from predators.

*Meerkats live in groups called **clans**. A few animals in each clan stand guard while the others play or look for food. If the guards see a predator, they warn the others with a loud bark. The others then run and hide in their underground homes. These babies are learning how to be guards.*

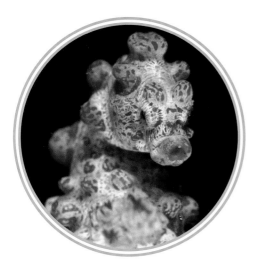

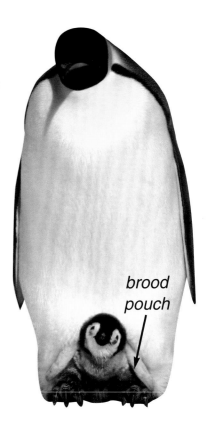

This emperor penguin father keeps his chick warm and safe in a **brood pouch** between his feet. The chick's mother has traveled far to find food. When the mother returns, she will feed her chick food that she brings up from her stomach. The chick's father then leaves to find food. The parents take turns feeding the chick and keeping it safe.

brood pouch

(above) This baby sea horse stays safe because other animals cannot see it in its ocean home. Its body blends in with the **coral** around it. Coral are ocean animals. Find the sea horse below.

coral

coral

This bear cub does not yet know why it should stay away from skunks. How will it learn? Do you think it will go near a skunk again? (See page 21.)

What are they saying?

Animals cannot speak the way we can, but they can **communicate**, or share information. Some animals, such as parrots, can **imitate**, or copy, human language and even understand some of the words they are saying.

Baby orangutans communicate using sounds and **gestures**, or movements. What might this baby be telling its mother?

Baby crocodiles call from their eggs to let the others in the nest know that it is time to hatch. By calling and hatching together, their mother is more likely to hear the babies and protect them from predators.

The best way a skunk communicates is through its bad smell. A skunk warns predators to stay away by growling, turning, and raising its tail. The skunk then sprays a very bad-smelling liquid from under its tail. Even baby skunks can spray. Pee-yew!

These young elephants are listening for **infrasound** calls made by other elephants. Infrasounds are low rumbling sounds that people cannot hear. To listen for messages sent, each elephant lifts a leg and faces the direction of the sound. Baby elephants also make these rumbling sounds to let their mothers know that they are hungry and want to nurse.

Learning from people

Baby pets are young animals that live with people. Caring for pets is a lot of work! Pets need to be fed, **groomed**, or cleaned, and exercised. They also need to learn how to live with people.

This girl is teaching her dog to sit. She uses her hand to show him what to do.

Training animals

Pets and many other animals are trained by people. Farm animals learn how to work and live on farms. Animals that take part in shows, such as dolphins and horses, are trained to do tricks to entertain people. Animals can learn to do many things.

This boy is holding a newborn kitten. Its cat mother will feed it for a few weeks, and then the boy will take care of it and teach it to be a good pet.

Dolphins are very smart animals that can be taught to do many tricks. These dolphins are giving this girl a ride on their backs.

This girl has taught her gray parrots many words and even a few songs. People who teach parrots to talk feel that these birds can understand many of the words they are saying.

People use horses for riding and pulling loads. Horses can also learn to race and jump over objects. This girl and her horse will take part in a jumping competition at a horse show.

Words to Know and Index

bodies
pages 7, 8, 10, 11, 17, 18, 19

communicating
pages 6, 20–21, 23

food
pages 6, 7, 10, 12–13, 14–15, 16, 17, 18, 19

hunting
pages 7, 12, 13, 14–15

keeping safe
pages 6, 7, 8, 9, 10, 18–19

migrating
pages 16–17

mothers
pages 7, 8–9, 10, 11, 12, 13, 14, 15, 16, 17, 18, 19, 20, 21, 22

Other index words

moving
pages 6, 7, 10–11

nursing
pages 8, 9, 12, 16, 21

people
pages 4–5, 21, 22–23